First published in Great Britain in 1998 by Macdonald Young Books

Macdonald Young Books,
an imprint of Wayland Publishers Ltd
61 Western Road
Hove
East Sussex
BN3 1JD

Text © Pat Thomas 1998
Illustrations © Lesley Harker 1998
Volume © Macdonald Young Books 1998

Editor: Lisa Edwards
Designer: Kate Buxton
Language consultant: Betty Root
Medical consultant: Dr Tony Smith

A CIP catalogue for this book is available from the British Library

Printed and bound in Portugal by Edições ASA

ISBN 0 7500 2574 3

Find Macdonald Young Books on the Internet
at http://www.myb.co.uk

My Amazing Journey

A FIRST LOOK AT WHERE BABIES COME FROM

PAT THOMAS
ILLUSTRATED BY LESLEY HARKER

MACDONALD YOUNG BOOKS

This is a story about you.
It is also a story about your mum
because once upon a time,
the two of you went on
an amazing journey.

Like all the best adventures
    it was exciting and difficult
    at the same time.

Everybody has had
this special adventure
with their mum,
and each adventure
is different.

7

Long before you lived here, you lived
in a very warm, dark place
inside your mum's body.
You were much
smaller then.

Have you ever
wondered how you
managed to get inside your mum?
Well, this is how it happened...

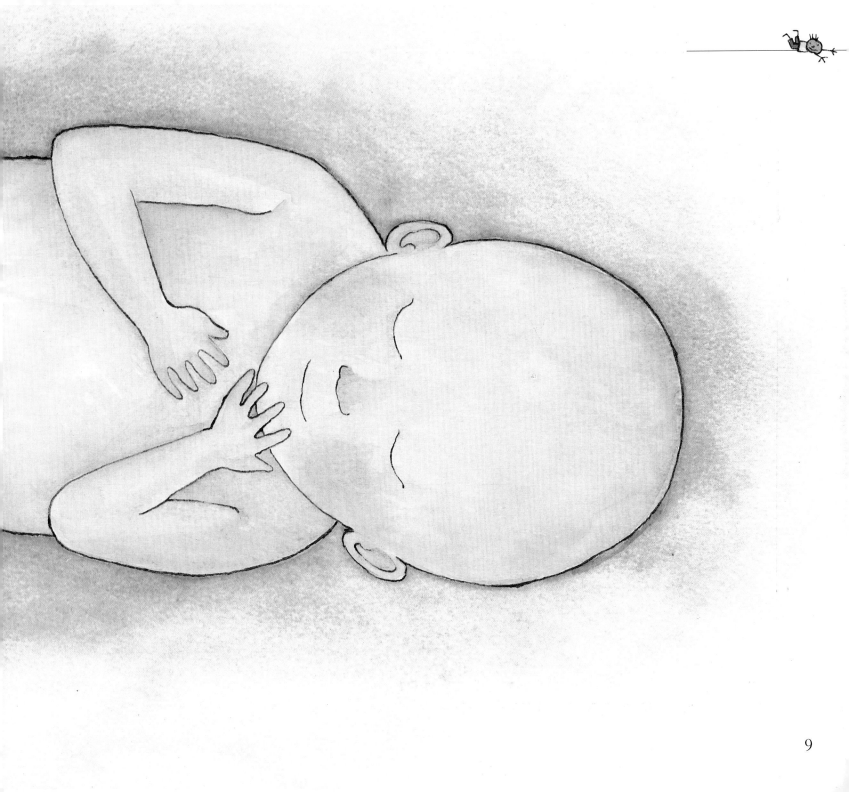

There are lots of ways
to tell someone that
you love them.

You can say it in words.

You can say it with a hug.

You can say it with flowers.

Another way grown-ups show someone that they love them is with their bodies. This is called making love.

Grown-ups make love because it feels nice,
to feel close to each other and to say 'I love you'.
They also make love when they want to make a baby.

KK170064

When two people want to make love
their bodies begin to change.

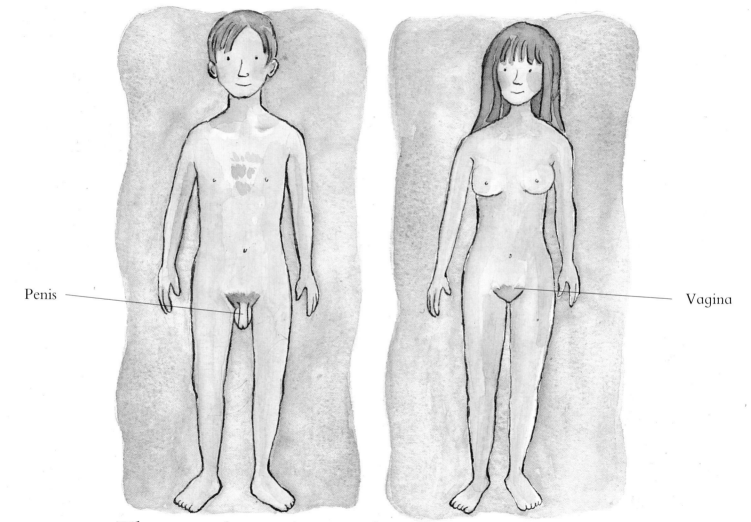

Penis

Vagina

The man's penis gets harder and longer and
the woman's vagina, inside her body, gets softer and bigger.

These changes make it easier for the man
to put his penis inside the woman.

The penis fits into the vagina like a finger fits into a glove.

One day, nine months before you were born,
your mum and dad made love.

After your dad
had moved his penis inside
your mum's vagina for a while,
it spurted out a warm liquid called
semen. In his semen were lots of tiny sperm.

Inside your mum was one egg. You started to grow when one of your dad's sperm planted itself in your mum's egg.

For the next nine months
you lived and grew inside your mum's body.
Your home was in her uterus.

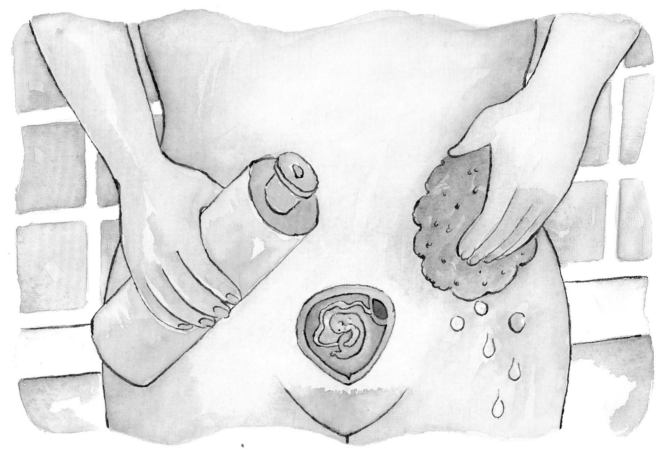

For about six weeks, you were so tiny that your mum
didn't even know you were there. But, from the beginning,
both of your bodies began to change and grow together.

After you had been inside your mum for two months
you had hands, feet, eyes, a nose and a mouth.

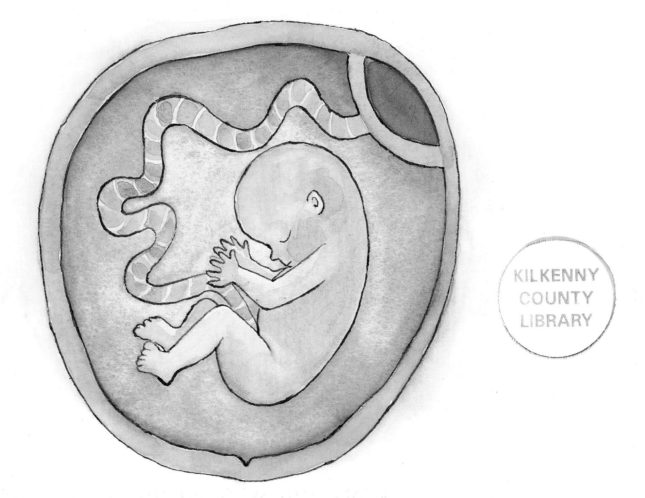

You were getting ready for the day
you would begin to live outside your mum's body.

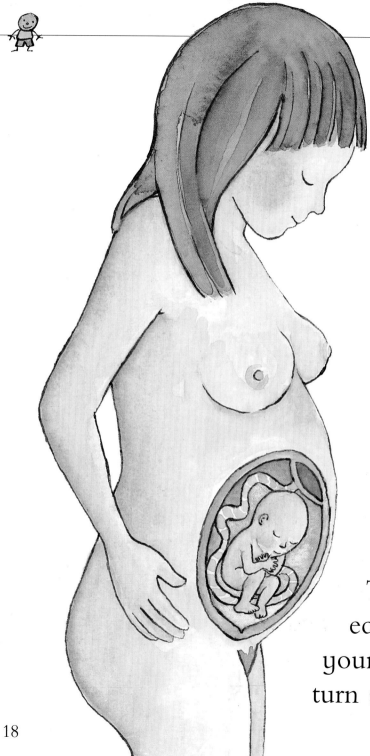

Inside your mum,
you were surrounded
by a warm liquid
which kept you safe.
This liquid made it
easy for you to move
your arms and legs and
turn somersaults.

All the time you were inside your mum you were joined to her by a long tube.

It was called the umbilical cord and it joined your body where your belly button is now. Everything your body needed to grow healthy and strong came through this tube.

After you had been inside your mum for four
or five months she could feel you kicking
and turning. This was very
exciting.

Not long after that,
other people could feel you kicking too.

Every sound your mum heard, you heard too.
Sometimes when your mum listened to music,
you moved around to it.

☀ What about you? 🏠

Have you ever talked to your
mum about the first time she felt
you kicking or heard
your heartbeat?

After about nine months you were big and strong enough to live out in the world.

Your mum's body began to change again, this time very quickly.

Her vagina started stretching to make it easier for you to get out.

At the same time, her uterus began getting smaller, helping to push you towards her vagina.

You and your mum had to work hard together to help you to be born. This work is called labour.

During labour, a midwife was there to check that you and your mum were all right. Your dad might have helped too.

Finally, you came out through your mum's vagina, into the world.

It was rather like pushing your head through a jumper.

Until that moment your mum could only imagine what you would be like. But after you were born your parents cuddled you and gave you a name.

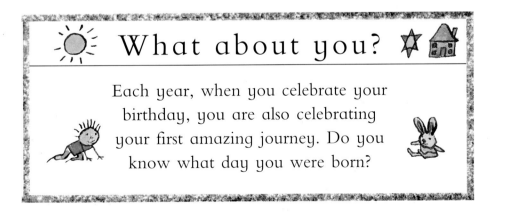

☀ What about you? ✡🏠

Each year, when you celebrate your birthday, you are also celebrating your first amazing journey. Do you know what day you were born?

Growing inside your mum, going through labour
and being born is an amazing journey.

And now that you are here, living in the world,
you will have many other amazing journeys
and many other exciting stories to tell...

...and each one will be as special as you are.

HOW TO USE THIS BOOK

It is a good idea to familiarize yourself with this book and think about some of
the questions/prompts contained within the text before you read it with a child. More than
just about the basics of reproduction, this book also talks about feelings and provides space
to consider the context in which sex, pregnancy and birth take place.

All children absorb information at a different rate and this book is meant to be read more than once.
Don't worry if some of the text seems to go over the child's head; when your child is ready he or she will
listen and understand the information. Equally, give the child time to ask questions in their own way.

Try to remember that the more at ease you can be when talking to a child about sex, the more confident
the child will become. Discussions which promote the idea that it is only for reproduction are sometimes
perceived as being easier, but they can cause problems later on when children begin to wonder about
sexual activity that does not result in a baby.

Girls are less likely than boys to be told the correct words for their reproductive organs. Try to avoid this
as it can have a negative impact on your child's confidence later in life. Also, girls need reassurance that
at the moment of birth, the vagina is naturally able to stretch open enough to allow the baby to come
out, and that after birth it can return to its normal size.

Little boys should understand that ejaculating is not the same as urinating. Although they both come out
of the same place, urine comes from a different part of the body. Sperm is made in the testicles and then
mixed with a fluid called semen before it is spurted out, or ejaculated. Ejaculation is a response to
pleasurable feelings of sexual contact.

One way to involve a child in learning about his or her birth is to make a special book which tells the
child's own story. It can include photos and drawings of parents and family members, mum when she was
pregnant, the newborn baby and the growing child. The child can be actively encouraged to participate
by sticking things in the book, drawing pictures and suggesting a commentary for each page.

GLOSSARY

Egg an egg in a woman's body is not like a chicken's egg. It has no hard shell and it is too small to be seen with your eyes. All the eggs in a woman's body are held in two small pouches called ovaries. Together, they hold around 500,000 eggs.

Penis the part of a man's body, between his legs, through which urine and semen pass.

Sperm when two people make love, millions of tiny sperm are spurted out through the penis in a fluid called semen. A baby starts to grow when one sperm plants itself inside a woman's **egg**.

Umbilical cord a long, bendy tube that connects a mother and her baby inside her tummy. The baby receives food and oxygen through the umbilical cord.

Uterus the safe place inside a mother's body where the baby grows until it is ready to be born. The uterus slowly gets bigger as the baby grows and then returns to its normal size after the baby is born. It is also known as the womb.

Vagina the passage that leads from the outside of a woman's body, between her legs, to the **uterus** inside her tummy.

FURTHER READING

How Did I Begin?
by Mick Manning and Brita Granström
(Franklin Watts, 1997)

How Do I Feel About? Our New Baby by Sarah Lavete
(Franklin Watts, 1997)

Me and My Body: Where Did I Come From?
by Claire Llewellyn and Mike Gordon
(Wayland Publishers, 1998)

Toppers: Babies by Nichola Baxter
(Franklin Watts, 1995)

Wonderwise: The World is Full of Babies
by Mick Manning and Brita Granström
(Franklin Watts, 1996)

Beginning Life by Geraldine Lux Flanagan
(Dorling Kindersley, 1996)

Being Born by Lennart Nilsson and Sheila Kitzinger
(Dorling Kindersley, 1996)

How are Babies Made? by Alastair Smith
(Usborne, 1997)